AUDIT OF THE DEPARTMENT OF JUSTICE'S HANDLING OF SEX OFFENDERS IN THE FEDERAL WITNESS SECURITY PROGRAM

EXECUTIVE SUMMARY*

In October 2011, the Department of Justice Office of the Inspector General (OIG) initiated an audit of the United States Marshal Service's (USMS) management of the Witness Security (WITSEC) Program. In May 2013, the Department of Justice (Department) Office of the Inspector General (OIG) issued a report examining the Department's handling of known or suspected terrorists in the Federal Witness Security (WITSEC) Program.[1] During that review, we identified sex offenders as another group of high-risk WITSEC Program participants (Program participants).[2] Therefore, we conducted this audit to evaluate the Department's: (1) admission and vetting of sex offenders into the WITSEC Program; (2) handling, tracking, and monitoring of sex offenders who were Program participants; and (3) procedures for notifying states, local municipalities, and other law enforcement agencies regarding the relocation of sex offenders.[3]

As of September 2014, the WITSEC Program (Program) has protected more than 8,648 witnesses and 9,967 of their dependants admitted into the Program since its inception in the early 1970's. In July 2013, at the onset of this portion of the WiTSec audit, the Department did not definitively know the number of sex offenders in the Program. As of July 2014, the Department had identified a total of 58 individuals who, at one point, were in the USMS WITSEC Program and are   sex offenders, including: (1) 10 individuals who were convicte o sex o enses prior to admittance, (2) 10 individuals who were convicted of a sex offense while in the Program, and (3) 38 individuals who were

---

* The full version of this report contains information that the Department of Justice considered to be law enforcement sensitive, and therefore could not be publicly released. To create this public version of the report, the Office of the Inspector General redacted (blacked out) portions of the full report.

[1] U.S. Department of Justice Office of the Inspector General, *Interim Report on the Department's Handling of Known or Suspected Terrorists Admitted into the Federal Witness Security Program*, Report 13-23 (May 2013).

[2] The Sex Offender Registration and Notification Act (SORNA) guidelines define a sex offender as "a person who was 'convicted' of a sex offense." SORNA establishes a national baseline for sex offender registration and notification programs, and generally constitutes a set of minimum national standards. SORNA does not limit a jurisdiction's discretion to adopt more extensive or additional registration and notification requirements.

[3] Our report is not intended to, and does not, assess the overall value or the processes that precede the admittance of convicted sex offenders into the Program, including the value of their testimony or cooperation.

convicted of a sex offense after being terminated from the Program.[4] Program officials further stated in July 2014 that there are no longer any active Program participants   .

The Department advised us that 38 of these 58 terminated Program artici ants are   , and ████████████████ . e Department further told us t at t e ot er 20 terminate Program participants are ████████████████ because they are either incarcerated, deceased, or have been deported; ████████████████████████████████████ .

We identified several significant concerns related to the Department's handling of known sex offenders who were once in the Program. Ten of the 58 sex offenders formerly in the Program were convicted sex offenders at the time of their admission into the Program.[5] Each of these individuals was convicted of a sex offense, such as rape or sexual assault of children.[6] Four of these 10 individuals received registration waivers at the time of their admission into the Program, ████ ██ We did not identify any instances where a sex offender, who had been granted a waiver of sex offender registration, was convicted of a new sex offense while in the Program. However, we believe that the Department generally did not utilize safeguards to protect and notify the public and law enforcement about the risk these individuals posed during the time period the waivers were in place.[7]

In addition, the Department informed us that individuals who were convicted of sex-related crimes   in the state of conviction or state of relocation have also been admitted into the Program. However, in May 2014, an official from the Criminal Division's Office of Enforcement Operations (OEO), which

---

[4] Individuals can terminate from the WITSEC Program voluntarily or may be terminated for cause. Throughout this report, we refer to active Program Participants as Program participants and refer to Program participants who have left the Program as "terminated."

The Department stated that none of these individuals, including the 38 individuals convicted of sex offenses after termination from the Program, were admitted into the Program based on a sex offense conviction.

[5] In November 2014, the Department stated that it should be noted that 4 of these 10 individuals were convicted of offenses prior to there being any legal requirement to reg ste (admissions were in 1961, 1967, 1968, and 1975) and prior to the passage of federal law that granted the Attorney General the authority to waive registration. In another instance, there was no legal requirement to register at the time of the offense or at the time of Program authorization. As of October 2014, Department officials advised us that all 58 identified individuals had been nformed of the ████████████████████████████ , as appropriate.

[6] One of the 10 individuals was convicted of more than one sex offense prior to entering the WITSEC Program.

[7] The Department stated law enforcement notification was made for one of the four individuals who received a waiver. The other individual was term nated from the Program prior to the Department being notified that the individual had a requirement to register as a sex offender.

authorizes the admission of individuals into the WITSEC Program, was unable to provide us with the number of active Program participants who met this description Then, in August 2014, the USMS informed us that at least four Program participants in good standing received a new name and had a sex offense ████████████ ████████████████████████████.[8] Given the nature of the WITSEC Program, we believe that individuals convicted of sex-related crimes ████████████████ ████████ pose risks that the Department needs to take into account and address. We believe that the Program must have strong policies in place to mitigate the public safety risk to vulnerable populations, such as children, posed by convicted sex offenders.

Through the course of our audit, we also learned about the anticipated release of four sex offenders from the Federal Bureau of Prisons (BOP) WITSEC Program by September 2018.[9] Upon release from prison, these individuals will be eligible for sponsorship into the WITSEC Program which may include relocation services and a new identity. Prior to late July 2014, neither OEO nor the USMS had finalized protocols in place for sex offenders admitted into the WITSEC Program and we recommended that each of them do so. OEO finalized a policy addressing this recommendation in late July 2014 and the USMS finalized their protocol in September 2014.

We believe the Department has not taken sufficient steps to mitigate the threat posed by Program participants, including sex offenders, who commit crimes after being terminated from the Program. For example, prior to late July 2014, the Department did not have a finalized policy for ensuring ████████████████ ██ █████████████████████ The ████████████ assists law enforcement officers in protecting the public and performing their official duties more safely by providing them with the information they need ████████████████████████████████. Because Program participants receive a new, government-provided identity upon entry to the Program, but are not monitored once they voluntarily or involuntarily terminate from the Program, we believe it is imperative that ████████████████ ██ ██████████████████████████████████████

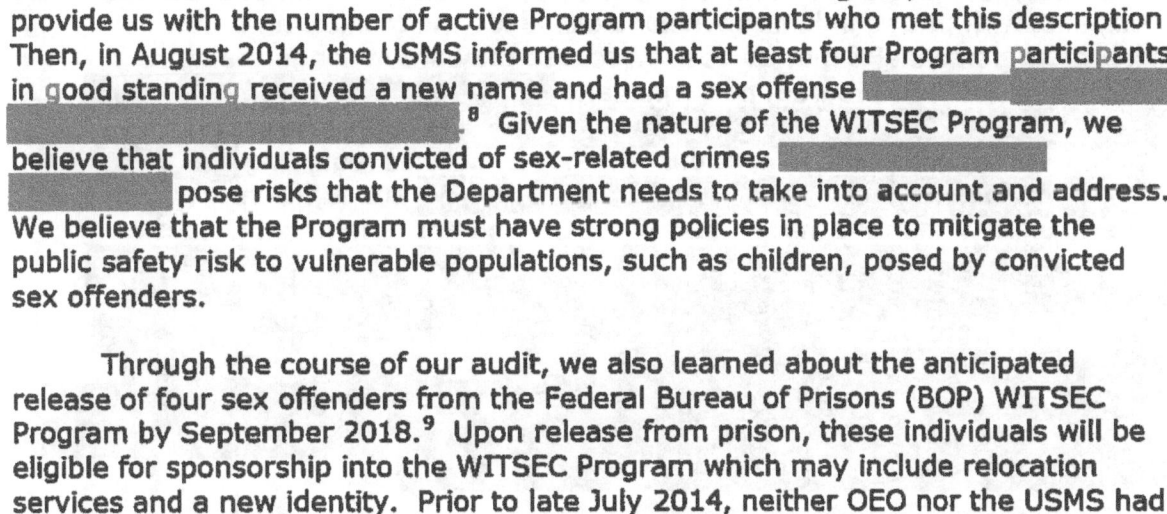

USMS Program personnel informed us that a total of 11,257 individuals have received a legal name change and subsequently left the Program.[10] We were also informed that almost ████████████ of these terminated Program participants – ████████████ - did not have ████████████ ████████████████████. While we recognize that not all of these terminated Program

---

[8] In good standing Program participants include funded individuals as well as those who are considered financially self-sufficient but still provided with security assistance.

[9] This audit does not assess the BOP's handling of Program participants who are convicted sex offenders and incarcerated.

[10] USMS officials informed us that these individuals have left the Program due to death, deportation, voluntary termination, or involuntary termination.

participants may have criminal histories, any one of these terminated Program participants with prior criminal convictions can elude the monitoring of law enforcement personnel if they so desire because they are no longer being monitored by WITSEC Program personnel and ███████████████████████ ██ Therefore, we believe that the Department needs to consider whether its policies regarding ████████ ████████████████████████████ are sufficient. We believe it is particularly important that all sex offenders who are terminated from the Program ██ ██ ███████. In the absence of ████████████████████████████████ ██ ██ ██ █████████████████████████████.

We make two recommendations to the Department to ensure that there are appropriate controls regarding Program participants who were convicted of sex offenses and that information is available to law enforcement on sex offenders and other Program participants with criminal histories who are no longer in the WITSEC Program.

AUDIT OF THE DEPARTMENT OF JUSTICE'S HANDLING OF SEX OFFENDERS IN THE FEDERAL WITNESS SECURITY PROGRAM

TABLE OF CONTENTS

Background Information 2

Program Admission Process... 2

Sex Offenders Admitted into the USMS WITSEC Program 3

   Convicted of a Sex Offense Prior to Program Participation   5

   Convicted of a Sex Offense During Program Participation... 7

   Convicted of a Sex Offense After Program Participation....   7

   Current Status of Sex Offenders... 8

Handling of Sex Offenders in the Program 10

   Waiver of Sex Offender Registration 10

   Sex Offender Residence 15

   Sex Offender Employment 15

   Law Enforcement Notification 16

OEO and USMS Protocols 18

▮▮▮▮▮▮▮▮▮▮▮▮▮▮▮▮ Terminated Program Participants
.... 20

Recommendations....... 24

STATEMENT ON INTERNAL CONTROLS....................... 25

STATEMENT ON COMPLIANCE WITH LAWS AND REGULATIONS   26

APPENDIX 1: OBJECTIVES, SCOPE, AND METHODOLOGY...... 27

APPENDIX 2: DEPARTMENT OF JUSTICE RESPONSE 30

APPENDIX 3: OIG ANALYSIS AND SUMMARY OF ACTIONS NECESSARY TO CLOSE THE AUDIT REPORT 35

AUDIT OF THE DEPARTMENT OF JUSTICE'S HANDLING OF SEX OFFENDERS IN THE FEDERAL WITNESS SECURITY PROGRAM*

In October 2011, the Department of Justice Office of the Inspector General (OIG) initiated an audit of the United States Marshal Service's (USMS) management of the Witness Security (WITSEC) Program. In May 2013, the OIG issued a report pertaining to the Department's management of known or suspected terrorists in the WITSEC Program. In 2012, during the course of that review, we identified another group of high-risk USMS WITSEC Program participants (Program participants), namely individuals convicted of sex offenses ██████████████ ████████████.[2] The objectives of this audit were to evaluate the Department's: (1) admission and vetting of sex offenders into the USMS WITSEC Program; (2) handling, tracking, and monitoring of sex offenders who were admitted into the USMS WITSEC Program; and (3) procedures for notifying states, local municipalities, and other law enforcement agencies regarding the relocation of sex offenders.

---

* The full version of this report contains information that the Department of Justice considered to be law enforcement sensitive, and therefore could not be publicly released. To create this public version of the report, the Office of the Inspector General redacted (blacked out) portions of the full report.

[1] See the OIG's report titled Interim Report on the Department's Handling of Known or Suspected Terrorists Admitted into the Federal Witness Security Program, US DOJ-OIG, Report 13-23, May 2013. See also: tt : www. u ti

[2] The Sex Offender Registration and Notification Act (SORNA) guidelines define a sex offender broadly, as "a person who was 'convicted' of a sex offense." SORNA establishes a national baseline for sex offender registration and notification programs and generally constitutes a set of minimum national standards. SORNA is not intended to preclude or limit jurisdictions' discretion to adopt more extensive or additional registration and notification requirements. Therefore, states ultimately establish the criteria, beyond these minimum standards, which must be met for an individual to be designated as a sex offender required to register. Federal law required the Attorney General to establish a national database by which the FBI could track certain offenders, the National Sex Offender Registry (NSOR), and directed states to participate in NSOR.

In 2012, after the 2011 Audit was initiated, the Department developed a definition for "sex offender" in order to identify sex offenders in the WITSEC Program. This definition provides that, for WITSEC Program purposes, a sex offender is an individual who was authorized for relocation and name change services who, rior to Pro ram authorization, was convicted of a sex offense for which the individual   ." Throughout this report, we refer to this group of individuals as   ." There may be Program participants who meet a state e nition o sex o en er ut not t e e nition designated by the Department for Program purposes.

[3] Our report is not intended to, nor does it, assess the overall value or the processes that precede the admittance of convicted sex offenders into the Program, including the value of their testimony or cooperation.

Background Information

The Federal WITSEC Program was authorized by the Organized Crime Control Act of 1970 and amended by the Comprehensive Crime Control Act of 1984. The Program is administered through three U.S. Department of Justice agencies: (1) the Criminal Division's Office of Enforcement Operations (OEO); (2) the USMS; and (3) the Federal Bureau of Prisons (BOP). OEO oversees the WITSEC Program (Program) by authorizing the admission of both incarcerated and non-incarcerated witnesses into the Program and, if necessary, terminating them from the Program. The USMS is responsible for relocating non-incarcerated witnesses and authorized dependants of that witness from danger areas so they may start a new life in a safe relocation area.[4] The BOP protects incarcerated Program participants as they serve their respective sentences, while the USMS protects incarcerated Program participants during travel for trial preparation and testimony. The focus of this audit is on OEO's and the USMS's administration of the USMS portion of the Program and does not review the BOP's handling of Program participants who are sex offenders and incarcerated.

As of September 2014, the Program has protected more than 8,648 witnesses and 9,967 of their family members admitted into the Program since its inception in the early 1970's. The makeup of Program participants has evolved over the years. While witnesses connected to the mafia and their criminal activities dominated the Program profile in its early years, the USMS has, in recent years, admitted an increasing number of witnesses associated with other types of organized crime cases, including some involved in violent gangs and terrorism. During this review, we found that some of these Program participants have been convicted of sex offenses[5]

Program Admission Process

To be admitted into the Program a federal prosecutor and an investigative agency must submit to OEO an application, risk assessment, and a threat

---

[4] Throughout the report, the witness, family members, and other dependants and associates will be referred to as Program participants. Danger areas are geographic areas that are deemed by the USMS to be a high threat area for the participants. A safe relocation area would be an area outside of the danger area.

[5] The Department stated that none of these individuals, including the 38 individuals convicted of sex offenses after termination from the Program, were admitted into the Program based on a sex offense conviction.

assessment on behalf of the witness.[6] Additionally, any participant 18 years of age or older undergoes a psychological evaluation performed by a ███████████████. Thereafter, the USMS conducts a preliminary interview with the applicant and informs OEO of the results, including a positive or negative recommendation for admittance into the Program. The OEO Director, as the Attorney General's designee, has the final authority to decide whether an applicant should be admitted into the Program and can override a USMS negative recommendation.

After OEO admits an applicant into the Program, USMS personnel obtain the Program participant's agreement to abide by Program rules through a Memorandum of Understanding (MOU). USMS WITSEC Program personnel create a new identity for Program participants and obtain new identity documentation.[7] Typically, the USMS assists witnesses and their dependants with ████████████████████ ████████████ determined to be essential for their security and assimilation into the community. ██ ████████████████████████.

At the conclusion of orientation, Program participants travel to the designated safe relocation area and begin their new life. In these geographic areas USMS WITSEC Inspectors assist new witnesses in becoming self-sufficient. Program assistance generally includes a monthly stipend for housing and living expenses, as well as vocational training and other necessary education. Program officials stated that the current Program policy recommends that WITSEC Program personnel initiate removal of funding 18 months after a Program participant has established a new identity or when a Program participant has achieved self-sufficiency.

Sex Offenders Admitted into the USMS WITSEC Program

Prior to 2012, the Department did not know the number of sex offenders admitted into the WITSEC Program, and we were unable to find any indication that the Department had attempted to identify the total population of sex offenders admitted into the Program.[8] According to officials, in 2012 OEO and the USMS began working together to determine the total number of sex offenders admitted

---

[6] National security stakeholders, such as the FBI and DEA, are nvolved in the Program admission process as sponsoring agencies. A sponsoring agency provides Program personnel with information on the witness, including a threat assessment and a risk assessment. The threat assessment evaluates the threat to the witness for cooperating with the federal government. The risk assessment reports on potential risks to the public caused by the witness' enrollment in the Program

[7] A witness's true identity refers to the name the witness had when he or she was admitted into the WITSEC Program. A witness's new identity refers to the name and identifying information provided by the government that replaces the individual's previous identity.

[8] The Department stated that, since 2004, there has been no individual authorized for relocation services who was ███████████████████████████ at the time of Program authorization.

into the Program, after the initiation of the 2011 OIG Audit of the WITSEC Program during which known or suspected terrorists and sex offenders were both identified as Program participants. However, in July 2013, approximately 2 years ater, the Department still could not definitively tell us the number of sex offenders admitted to the Program. In order to determine the number of sex offenders admitted to the Program, the Department had to first create and agree upon its definition of the term "sex offender" for Program purposes. A USMS officia stated that a meet'ng was held in June 2013 to determine the WITSEC Program definition for "sex offender." The Department provided documentation dated July 16, 2013, which noted the agreed upon definition as, "an individual who was authorized for relocation and name change services, who, prior to authorization, was convicted of a sex offense ███ ██."

Although the USMS and OEO agreed on a Program specific definition of sex offender, determining which Program participants were ████████████████████ ███████████████████████ proved to be a challenge for the Department. We found that the Department took several steps in its endeavor to identify the total number of sex offender participants in the Program. In October 2012, the USMS compared Program identity information (old names, new names, and any aliases) for the approximately 54,000 names used by all Program participants over the age of 10 ███████████████████████████████████████. After completing the comparison, USMS Program personnel utilized the USMS's Nationa Sex Offender Targeting Center Sex Offender Investi ations Branch SOIB to assist in the   rocess of determinin

                                                                       .   personne

contacte   on a case-   -case   asis to determine case
dispositions

As a result of the comparison in October 2012, as well as a manual review of OEO and USMS case files, the Department, as of July 2014, identified 58 individuals who, at some point in time, had been admitted into the WITSEC Program ████████

████████████████████████.[10] These 58 individuals fall into 3 categories - participants who were convicted of a sex offense committed prior to, during, or after Program participation. OEO and USMS officials stated in July 2013, and reaffirmed in July 2014, that there were no longer any active Program participants ████████████████████████ in the Program.[11]

Convicted of a Sex Offense Prior to Program Participation

Ten terminated Program participants who were convicted of sex offenses, such as rape and sexual assault of children, prior to Program admission ██

██

████████.[12]

---

[10] We judgmentally selected for review 21 of the 47 sex offender files that had been identified by OEO and the USMS as of 2013. This judgmental sample was based on the July 2013 lists of identified sex offenders who had been admitted into the WITSEC Program and included: all 8 of the files for individuals who had sex offense convictions at the time of their admittance to the Program; all 8 of the files for individuals who were convicted of a sex offense ████████████████ while in the Program; and 5 of the 31 files for individuals who were convicted of a sex offense ██████████████████████ after being either voluntarily or involuntarily terminated from the Program. Subsequent to our review, OEO provided the OIG with numerous updated lists of the sex offenders it had identified. The most recent list from July 2014, approximately 1 year after the audit was initiated, includes a total of 58 individuals. We did not perform a review of the additional files Please see Appendix I for more information about the judgmental sample and WITSEC Program file review.

[11] An active Program participant is defined as a person who has been authorized into the Program and has not been precluded from further financial or protective services through their termination from the Program. Individuals can terminate from the Program voluntarily or may be terminated for cause. A Program participant who willfully commits an act in violation of their Program agreement may be terminated for cause. Throughout this report, we refer to active Program participants as Program participants and refer to Program participants who have left the Program as "terminated" Program participants.

In addition to the 58 individuals identified, a sex offender applicant who was in the process of seeking admission into the Program as of January 2014 was denied admission to the Program by OEO.

[12] One of the 10 individuals was convicted of more than one sex offense prior to entering the WITSEC Program.

- Four of these 10 individuals received a waiver of sex offender registration from the Department.[13]

  ██████████████████████████████████████ by the Department in October 2012, at which time two of these participants decided to voluntarily terminate from the Program. The third individual had been terminated from the Program prior to October 2012.

  The fourth individual was identified as a sex offender in March 2013 as a result of the manual review of OEO's case files, and the participant's ██████████████████████████████ in April 2013. This Program participant had been terminated from the Program in November 2003.

  Following the Department's ████████████████████ in 2012 and 2013, three of these individuals ███████████████████████████ ██████████ and Department documentation from July 2013 noted that the fourth ████████████████████████████████████ in the ███ ████████████ in 2011. However, according to Department documentation received in May 2014, the fourth ██████████████ ██████████████████████████████ According to the Department, OEO authorized disclosure of this terminated Program participant's identity to officials in the state of relocation and USMS officials reported that   .

- One of these 10 terminated Program participants was admitted after the passage of the Wetterling and Adam Walsh Acts but was not believed to ████████████████████████████████████ at the time of Program authorization. However, nearly 2 years after this individual was removed from the Program, ████████████████████ ███ ████████████. The Department stated that it not'fied this individual ████████ and that he subsequently moved to an area ██ .

---

[13] The WITSEC statute and the Sex Offender Registration and Notification Act (SORNA) guidelines allow for the waiver of sex offender registration requrements in the interest of a protected witness's safety. However, both the WITSEC statute and SORNA gu de ines state that the risks posed to the relocation communities by these protected individuals must be considered by the Attorney General or his or her designee. 18 U S.C § 3521(b)(1)(H) (2011) and 18 U S.C. § 3521. The waivers reviewed by OIG auditors in the course of th s audit were executed by the Attorney General's designee at the time.

In November 2014, the Department stated that it should be noted that 4 of these 10 individuals were convicted of offenses prior to there being any legal requirement to register (admissions were in 1961, 1967, 1968 and 1975) and prior to the passage of federal aw that granted the Attorney General the authority to wa ve registration. In another instance, there was no legal requirement to register at the time of the offense or at the time of Program authorization. As of October 2014, Department officials advised us that all 58 identified individuals had been nformed █ ████████████████████████████████████ , as appropriate

- The remaining five terminated Program participants were authorized into the Program prior to the passage of sex offender registration legislation. All of these individuals were removed from the Program prior to or within the same year as the passage of the Wetterling Act in 1994, the statute that established guidelines for states to track sex offenders.[14]

In July 2014, OEO provided information confirming ████████████████████████████████ in the group ████████████████. At that time, one individual had been informed ████████████████, but the Department was unable to verify ████████████. Department officials informed us that this individual had been ████████████, in late October 2014. For the remaining two individuals, one moved to an area where ████████████████████ and the other is incarcerated.

Convicted of a Sex Offense During Program Participation

Ten terminated Program participants had no ████████████████████████ at the time of their admission into the Program, but were convicted of a sex offense ████████████████ while in the Program.[15]

- The Department stated that all 10 of these Program participants were terminated from the Program as a result of being arrested or convicted of a sex offense ████████████████████.

- Of these 10 sex offenders, 1 is deceased and 3 are incarcerated. The Department states that it has confirmed ████████████████ for the other six individuals.

Convicted of a Sex Offense After Program Participation

Thirty-eight Program participants had no ████████████████████████ at the time of their admission into the Program or during their time in the

---

[14] We found no documentation to support that, prior to 2012, the Department revisited the issue of ████████████ for four of these five individuals after the passage of the Wetterling Act in 1994 or after the ████████████████████ were made retroactive by 28 C.F.R. Part 72 in February 2007.

[15] We note that one of the individuals from the list of identified sex offenders with a sex offense conviction ████████████████ prior to admission into the Program also qualifies for the list of individuals who were convicted of a sex offense ████████████ while in the Program. This individual was a juvenile when he was authorized into the Program in 1995. However, he was terminated from the Program in April 2001 based on the serious nature of the sex offense he was charged with while in the Program in addition to a prior incident of the same nature. This sex offender was then reinstated into the Program in November 2002, ████████████████████ ████████████, a new identity, and was relocated in order to be reunited with his father who had recently been released from prison and authorized into the WITSEC Program. While there ████████████████ ████████████████████████████████████, there was no indication in the WITSEC Program file that law enforcement notification was made in any of the subsequent relocation areas.

Program, but were convicted of a sex offense ███████████████ after termination from the Program.[16]

- The Department stated that it has confirmed ███████████████ for 23 of these 38 Program participants. According to the Department, 14 individuals are currently deceased, incarcerated, or have been deported.

- According to documentation obtained from the Department in July 2014, ██████████ for the remaining individual had not yet been confirmed. In October 2014, Department officials informed us that this individual had been ████████████████████

Current Status of Sex Offenders

In July 2014, documentation from the Department indicated ████████ ████████████████████ for all but 2 of the 58 identified individuals had been confirmed as ██.[17] However, in October 2014 the Department confirmed that all 58 had been ████████████████████████████

In April and May 2014, OIG auditors conducted an independent verification of ██ for both the ████████████████████████ of each of the individuals in our sample. ⌐ We were unable to locate records for every participant and many of the records we found did not account for ████████████████████████. However, in July 2014 USMS officials informed OIG auditors that ████████████████████ should not be used as a tool to verify ████████████████████████ because it does not include all of the ████████████ ████████████████████ that is made available to law enforcement

---

[16] It should be noted that almost half of these 38 individuals entered the Program as minors (under the age of 18) and more than 10 of them also left the Program as minors. Additionally, while 37 of these 38 individuals have been terminated from the WITSEC Program, one is in the Program as a prisoner witness serving a life sentence.

[17] Prior to July 2014, the Department noted that the ████████████████████ in the state of conviction ██████████ for one individual for whom ██████████████ had previously not been confirmed. As of May 2014, the Department's information indicated that this individual ██████████████████████████ and that OEO had authorized disclosure ████████████████████████ OEO previously ████████████████████████████ for this individual ██████████████. In July 2014, Department officials provided documentation that this individual ████████████████████ ████████████████████.

One of the two individuals for whom ████████████████████████████ as of July 2014 indicated to WITSEC Program personnel ████████████████████████████████, which is based on a ████████████████████. The ████ ████████████████████████████████ for sexual intercourse with a female under the age of 16, whom he later married and divorced. As of October 2014, the Department confirmed that this individual ████████████████████.

18

personnel ████████████████████.[19] Given the discrepancy between public and law enforcement █████████████████████, we recommend that the Department confirm that all sex offenders previously admitted into the Program ██ to mitigate the risk to the public.[20] In November 2014, Department officials informed us that they ███████████████ of all identified terminated Program ████████████████. As discussed in the ██████████ section of this report, we believe that any future sex offenders admitted into the Program who are █████████████ and who are terminated from the Program should be required to abide by the above mentioned criteria.

In addition to the 58 individuals already identified by the Department, there were at least 15 convicted sex offenders in federal custody, as of May 2014, who were in the BOP WITSEC Program, 4 of whom are anticipated to be released by September 2018. Upon release from prison, BOP WITSEC Program participants are eligible for sponsorship into the WITSEC Program and may receive name change and relocation services if accepted into the Program. USMS officials stated that participation in the BOP WITSEC Program does not automatically grant individuals access into the USMS WITSEC Program. However, these individuals may be sponsored into the Program and receive relocation and name change services upon release from prison, which increases the likelihood that WITSEC Program officials will be confronted with the issue of whether or not to admit a sex offender into the Program and, if so, how to handle and monitor such a participant.[21]

The Department informed us that, as of April 2014, OEO and the USMS have completed an initial screening of every WITSEC Program case file and files flagged as having a possible link to a sexual offense have been referred for additional review of ████████████████████. Yet, as of May 2014, an OEO official stated that he was unable to readily provide us with the number of Program participants who were in good standing and convicted of at least one sex-related offense ████████████████████████████████████.[22] In August 2014, the USMS informed us that at least four Program participants in good standing received a new name and had a sex offense ████████████████████████████ ████████████. We believe that individuals convicted of sex-related offenses ██████

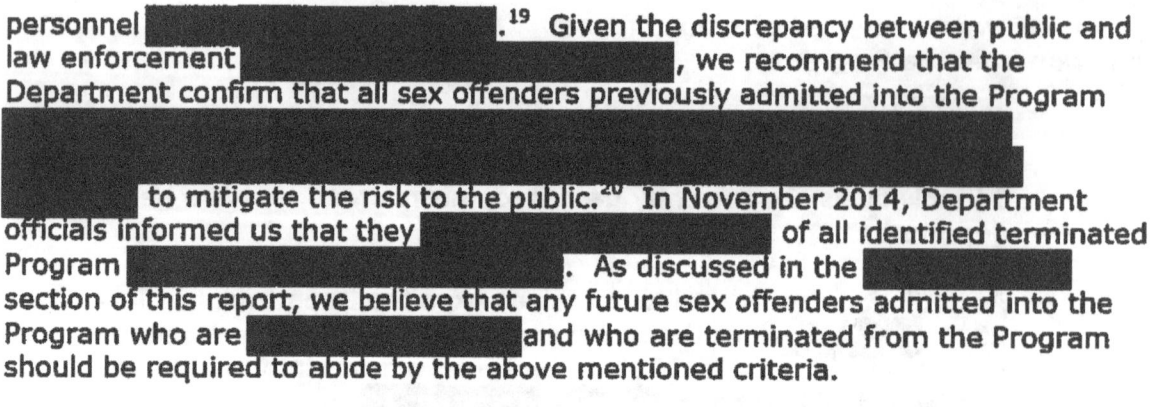

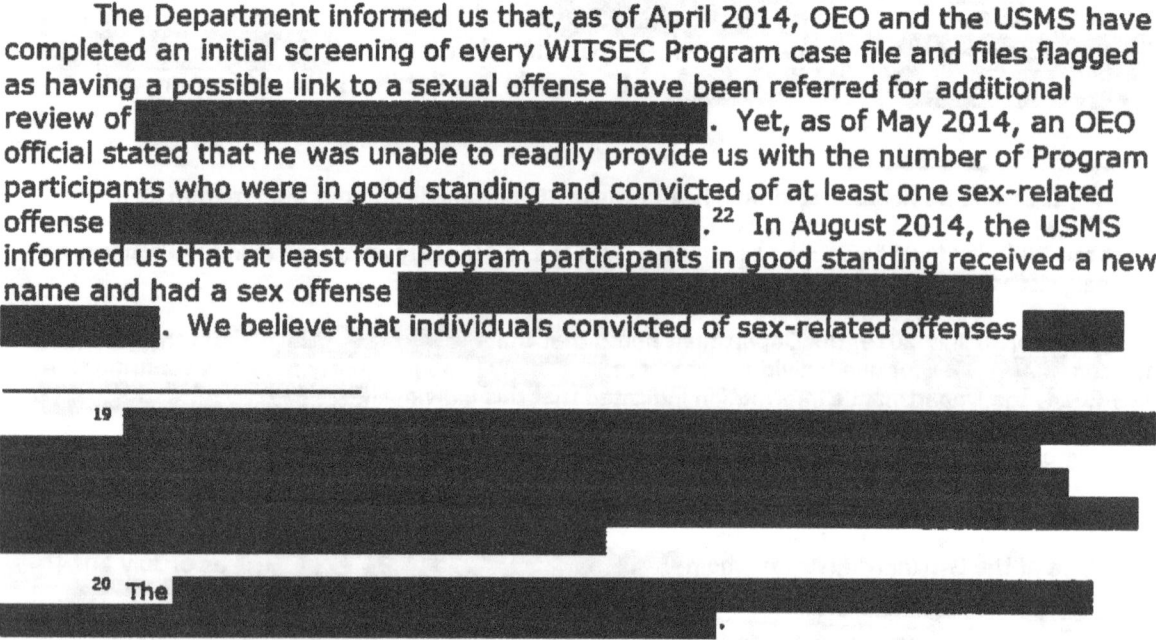

[21] As discussed below, this highlighted the need for a finalized OEO protocol that addresses the eligibility of such persons to the WITSEC Program.

[22] In good standing Program participants include those who are funded as well as participants who are considered financially self-sufficient but still provided with security assistance.

██████████████████████ pose risks that the Department needs to take into account and address.

The list of ███████████████████████████████████ that is maintained by the Department has changed during this audit ██. For example, an individual who was on the July 2013 list of Program participants as having been convicted of a sex offense ████████████████ ████████████ prior to his admission to the Program has since been removed from the list ███. OIG auditors found no indication that these individuals are tracked once they are removed from the list. We believe that identifying and maintaining a current list of all current Program participants who have been convicted of a sex-related crime would allow the Department to keep better track of Program participants with a sex-related criminal history and put the Department in a better position to determine a participant's ██████████████████████ at any given time ████████████████████. We further believe that maintaining current up-to-date records for these individuals would allow the Department to evaluate the risks these individuals pose to the public, thereby enabling it to ensure the appropriate handling and monitoring of these Program participants.

We believe that the Department has made significant efforts since 2012 to identify all sex offenders admitted into the Program through ████████████████ ████ the case file review. However, by limiting their identification to only those individuals who ████████████████████████████, OEO and the USMS have not ensured that they have identified all individuals who may pose a risk and were admitted into the Program. In order to ensure that all individuals are appropriately identified and handled in the USMS WITSEC Program, we recommend that OEO and the USMS identify all individuals currently active in the Program who have been convicted of a sex-related crime in order to be in a position to properly mitigate the risks associated with these individuals.

Handling of Sex Offenders in the Program

Although there were no active Program ████████████████████████ ████████████ as of July 2014, we have significant concerns related to the Department's handling of the identified sex offenders that were formerly in the Program. In particular, we are concerned about the Department's granting of waivers of sex offender registration, where the Department relocated these individuals while in the Program, how employment of sex offenders was handled, and the failure to notify law enforcement about a sex offender's relocation to their community.

Waiver of Sex Offender Registration

As noted above, the Department thus far has identified 10 individuals who were convicted sex offenders at the time of their admission into the Program. Each of these individuals was convicted of a sex offense, such as rape of a child or sexual assault. Four of these 10 individuals received sex offender registration waivers from OEO at the time of their admission to the Program, ████████████████████ ████████████████████.[23]

The WITSEC statute provides that the Attorney General may, by regulation:

> ...protect the confidentiality of the identity and location of persons subject to registration requirements as convicted offenders under Federal or State law, including prescribing alternative procedures to those otherwise provided by Federal or State law for registration and tracking of such persons.[24]

We reviewed federal sex offender registration laws and regulations, including the Wetterling Act (1994), Megan's Law (1996), the Adam Walsh Act (2006), and the Sex Offender Registration and Notification Act (SORNA) Guidelines published by the DOJ in July 2008. The Wetterling Act, Megan's Law, and the Adam Walsh Act address federal sex offender registration requirements and the public dissemination of state sex offender registries' information. The SORNA Guidelines were issued by the Department to interpret and implement Title I of the Adam Walsh Act, more commonly known as SORNA. We found that the SORNA Guidelines encourage jurisdictions to make provisions in their laws and procedures to accommodate consideration of the security of protected individuals and to honor requests from the USMS and other agencies responsible for witness protection in order to ensure that the witness's security is not compromised.

While both the WITSEC statute and the SORNA Guidelines provide for the exclusion of protected witnesses from registration requirements, the WITSEC statute further states that the "Attorney General shall also make a written assessment in each case of the seriousness of the investigation or case in which the person's [assistance] has been or will be provided and the possible risk of danger to other persons and property" in the relocation community and "... determine whether the need for that person's testimony outweighs the risk of danger to the public."

---

[23] Another 5 of these 10 individuals were not legally ████████████████ at the time of Program authorization and entered the Program prior to the passage of federal law that granted the Attorney General the authority to waive registration. The remaining individual was authorized into the Program after the passage of the Wetterling Act but the state of conviction did not nform the Department of this individual's ██████████████████ until July 2013, over a year after the individua was terminated from the Program. As of October 2014, Department officials advised us that all 58 identified individuals had been informed of ████████████████ and ████████████ , as appropriate.

[24] 18 U.S.C. § 3521(b)(1)(H) (2006). The provision in the WITSEC statute that prov ded the Attorney General with the authority to waive sex offender registration did not take effect until November 1997 when Congress passed Public Law 105-119. Therefore 5 of the 10 individuals identified by the Department as having been convicted of a sex offense, for which ████████████ ███████, prior to Program admission, were not eligible for a waiver of sex offender registration.

[25] 18 U.S.C. § 3521(c) (2006).

During our audit, we found that OEO granted waivers of sex offender registration for individuals upon admission to the Program and that these waivers, with one exception ███ ." We believe that the waiver memorandum language appeared to ██ in the Program participant's relocation area, and was focused solely on the safety considerations of the Program participant.[26] This language does not incorporate the language from the WITSEC statute, which provides that, where registration is determined not to be appropriate, alternative procedures may be coordinated. We believe that a waiver of the registration requirement with no alternative procedures in place to monitor these individuals does not strike a balance between the safety of the witness and the risk to the public, but instead elevates the security of the witness over the risk to the public. During the course of this audit, in June 2014, we recommended that OEO finalize a protocol containing criteria to assist current and future OEO officials in determining whether or not to issue a waiver of registration and whether or not to notify law enforcement of these individuals' placements into relocation communities. In July 2014, we further recommended that the USMS finalize a protocol to ensure the appropriate handling and monitoring of sex offenders admitted into the Program. These recommendations were important as the implementation would provide a more formalized and comprehensive analysis prior to authorization of these individuals into the Program and provide for the comprehensive handling and monitoring procedures once a sex offender is admitted into the Program. In late July and September 2014, OEO and the USMS, respectively, finalized policies addressing these recommendations.

As illustrated by Table 1 below, OEO originally granted waivers for 4 of 10 sex offenders admitted into the Program. After the initiation of the OIG's audit in October 2011, ███████████████████████████████████████ For the first seven individuals listed in Table 1, we found only one instance where there was documentation showing that law enforcement was notified about the presence of the individual in the relocation community. Although notification of the first relocation was timely, notification of the individual's second relocation was not made until approximately 4 years after it occurred.[27]

---

[26] The actual language found in half of OEO's waivers of sex offender registration was: "…please arrange for … ██ ██████. If they do not, pursuant to Title 18, United States Code, Section 3521(b)(1)(H), I am hereby waiving the requirement…."

[27] At the time of our testing the Department had only informed us of eight individuals who had been convicted of a sex offense prior to admission into the Program. In July 2014, the Department provided updated information reflecting that 1 individual had been removed from the list and 3 individuals added, resulting in a total of 10 individuals listed in this group. We did not test the WITSEC Program files for the additional three individuals identified on the July 2014 list and, therefore, did not determine whether law enforcement was notified in these cases.

T ble 1

OEO Waiver of Sex Offender Registration
for Sex Offenders Admitted into the Program[28]

i   r

May 1980; reauthorized into Program following me conspiracy to commit mail ud in y 1983	1976 - Rape	No	W not requi to register at the time of Program admission; th I ividual's adm n a val m the Program predated reg on I islation by at least 9 years and p ted the Attorney General' uthority to waive registration by at least 12	N/A
June 1993	1989 - Sodomy	No	No discussion of registration at the time of Program admission. This individual was admitted prior to the Wetterling Act and the Attorney General's authority to waive registration by approximately 4 years.	N/A
July 2004	1985 – Rape of Child with Force; Sodomy Solicitation 1 [30]	Yes	N/A	
November 2001	1999 Sexual Assault	Yes	N/A	▮▮▮▮
June 2002	1988 – Lewd or Lascivio Acts with Child Under	Yes	A	▮▮▮▮
October 1995; rei stated into Progra llowi	2001 – Crimina	Yes		

---

[28] This table does not list Sex Offender (SO) 6 as OEO removed the individual from this group in May 2014.

[29] In addition to the individuals listed in Table 1, the Department issued a registration waiver to one additional Program participant. However, the Department confirmed with state authorities in 2013 that this individual was not ▮▮▮▮▮▮▮▮▮▮▮▮▮▮▮▮▮. Therefore, while a waiver was issued, he was not included in any of the Department's lists of identified sex offenders throughout this audit.

[30] Department information indicates that this individual was also arrested in 1990 for Sodomy, Solicitation, and Public Indecency - Indecent Exposure; but that the disposition of that arrest is unknown.

a conviction for a offense	Sexua Conduct		N/A	████
n Novem 2002				
March 2011	1998 – Acting in a Manner to Injure a Child under 17 and Sexual Abuse		OEO was not notified of this sex offender's registration requirement until almost 2 years after his removal from the Program.	N/A
April 1978	1961 – Sexual Intercourse with a Female under 16		This individual was admitted approximately 19 years prior to Congress enacting legislation providing the Attorney Genera with the authority to waive registration.	N/A
September 1979	1967 - Rape		This individual was admitted approximately 18 years prior to Congress enacting legislation providing Attorney Genera with the authority to waive registration.	N/A
July 1979	1968 – Sodomy		This individual was admitted approximately 18 years prior to Congress enacting legislation providing the Attorney Genera with the authority to waive registration.	N/A

Source: Office of Enforcement Operations.

As referenced above, in June 2014, we recommended that OEO fnalize a written protocol that contains criteria to assist current and future OEO officials in determining whether or not to issue a waiver for requiring registration of sex offender Program participants. Draft OEO protocols acknowledged the risk to the public of such registration waivers and included criteria to be considered in deciding whether or not to grant a waiver of the sex offender registration requirement for individuals who were ███████████████████████████ prior to admission into the Program. OEO finalized a protocol in late July 2014 which states that, because of the risks to the public associated with waiving registration requirements, there is a presumption against admitting sex offenders ████████ ██████████████████████ into the Program.[31] We believe the inclusion of decision-making criteria in the OEO protocol will be useful to current and future OEO officials in determining whether or not to grant a waiver of sex offender registration requirements.

---

[31] This finalized protocol was later amended on September 5 2014, and again on November 5, 2014. Both of these revised OEO protocols have retained the language regarding criteria to assist OEO officials in determining whether or not to issue a waiver for sex offender registration of Program participants.

Sex Offender Residence

As of July 2014, there was no specific Program policy requiring USMS WITSEC Inspectors to take statutory residency prohibitions into consideration when determining the appropriateness of a sex offender Program participant's residence within the relocation community. We believe this is concerning because relocating a sex offender, especially a sex offender who targets a specific type of victim, to certain areas may place the Program participant in close proximity to locations with vulnerable individuals that should be avoided, such as playgrounds, day care centers, and schools. In the course of our audit, we determined that the USMS did not retain accurate address information for sex offender Program participants who, but for their participation in the Program, would otherwise have been required to register as sex offenders. Thus, we were unable to review case file documentation to determine if the USMS had unknowingly or inappropriately relocated sex offenders to high risk areas.

We believe that residence decisions for sex offender Program participants are especially important when sex offender registration requirements are waived and the individuals are provided with new identities with no notification of their sex offense history to law enforcement in their area of relocation. We further believe that without implementing law enforcement safeguards or instituting preventive measures to mitigate the risks, these types of circumstances provide a clear opportunity for an individual to recidivate in a relocation community. We believe these are unnecessary risks to the public that the Department must address. In July 2014, we recommended that the USMS finalize a protocol that specifically addresses appropriate restrictions on where sex offender Program participants can reside, work, and go to school to help mitigate risks posed by these individuals in the relocation community. We also recommended that the USMS document Program participants' compliance. In September 2014, the USMS finalized a protocol that addresses the procedure for identifying and complying with restrictions for sex offenders admitted into the WITSEC Program.

Sex Offender Employment

We have similar concerns about certain types of jobs, such as those working with or in close proximity to vulnerable individuals such as children, which sex offender Program participants should not hold based on the potential safety concerns that these individuals pose. We view employment by sex offenders admitted into the Program as a high-risk issue that necessitates greater oversight. As of July 2014 there were no finalized Program policies specific to the monitoring and approval of sex offender Program participant employment by USMS WITSEC Program Inspectors, regardless of whether or not the USMS assisted the individual in obtaining the employment.

In general, USMS WITSEC Program Inspectors are aware of the employment obtained by active Program participants because employment and self-sufficiency are linked to how long a Program participant continues to receive Program funding. Moreover, USMS WITSEC Program personnel will, at times, assist the Program participant in obtaining gainful employment. It is common practice for Program participants to be ██ ████████████████████████████ This is because the ████████ ███ ███ While this is an important safeguard for all witnesses, some occupations that place individuals in a position of trust within a community may not require ████████████████████████████. Therefore, if a sex offender Program participant is not ████████████ and is also granted a waiver of registration, there are no safeguards in place to alert the public to the individual's criminal history.

We believe that employment of a sex offender Program participant, who receives a new identity, requires USMS WITSEC Program personnel oversight, especially when OEO waives sex offender registration and does not authorize law enforcement notification. In the course of our audit, we did not identify any instances where a sex offender was admitted into the Program and provided a new identity, relocated, and granted a waiver of sex offender registration and then was convicted of a new sex offense while in the WITSEC Program. Nonetheless, we believe this situation provides the individual with an opportunity to recidivate, while not being required to adhere to the legally mandated safeguards or preventative measures.

Law Enforcement Notification

Another method of mitigating risk to the public is notifying law enforcement of the sex offender Program participant's relocation to the community. ████████ ███ ██████████████████████████████████████ law enforcement notification provides information only to the appropriate law enforcement officials. Law enforcement notification generally includes verbal information on the sex offender's relocation to the area of jurisdiction, the offender's previous criminal history, and coordination with Program personnel on any investigation of a sex crime. As the Attorney General's delegate, the Director of OEO maintains the authority to authorize such notification of Program information.

While WITSEC Program officials have expressed concerns over the potential for corrupt law enforcement officials to breach a witness's security as a result of law enforcement notification, based on our review of an OEO memorandum from November 1996, we learned that as early as the 1980's OEO initiated a voluntary policy of law enforcement notification for certain relocated witnesses, including those with a history of sexual crimes. A 1996 memorandum acknowledges that while notification of law enforcement increases the risk of danger to the witness, "... the ever-increasing violent nature of many of the witnesses entering the Program ... has forced [OEO] to significantly increase notification to law enforcement." OEO has authorized law enforcement notification on a case-by-case basis due to risks these witnesses presented to the areas of relocation.

According to USMS policy, Program personnel shall comply with OEO's authorization to notify state and law enforcement agencies of the presence of any Program participant convicted of crimes of violence, sexual offenses, and major narcotics distribution. If this authorization is granted, USMS policy requires that Program personnel meet with appropriate law enforcement officials and notify them of the presence of a Program participant in their jurisdiction within 10 business days of the Program participant obtaining permanent housing. Law enforcement authorities are provided a verbal summary of the Program participant's criminal history, the Program participant's new name and address, and whether or not the Program participant is on supervised release.[32]

In August 2007, OEO issued another memorandum in which it reviewed its law enforcement notification policy. This memorandum was issued in response to USMS concerns that the then-current process of notification was insufficient for effective use by law enforcement agencies. The August 2007 memorandum more clearly states that the USMS will execute law enforcement notification only when it is expressly mandated in the OEO letter of authorization and only under certain egregious circumstances.

During our Program file review, we found that OEO had authorized law enforcement notification for 2 of the 10 sex offenders who were admitted into the Program.[33] For one of these individuals, OEO authorized notification to the State sex offender registration officials but the participant was removed from the Program and relocated himself to a different area prior to notification. OIG auditors found no evidence that notification to State sex offender registration officials was completed prior to the individual's move. However, WITSEC Program officials stated that notification was made with the State regist   in the second location. This individual eventually moved once more to an area

For the second of these individuals, the notification authorization letter dated in 2004 states that the notification was authorized based on a history of crimes of violence, including the rape of a child   ith force. USMS officials informed the OIG that notification was made to law enforcement in February 2005 in the relocation area. However, we obtained from OEO a 2007 memorandum in which OEO waived the notification of law enforcement based on the be ief that notification "... would pose an extreme detriment to the safety of the witness," and the file indicated that this individual subsequent y moved with USMS permission in April 2008. We found no documentation that law enforcement notification was executed in this new area until September 2012 despite this individual being funded by the WITSEC Program until 2012. In August 2012, the Director of OEO issued a memorandum authorizing law enforcement notification of t 's individual's presence in the community and law

---

[32] Any additional information re uested by law enforcemen officials requires the approval of USMS headquarters personnel.

[33] The Department stated that only one of these two indiv duals was provided a waiver of sex offender registration. The other individual was terminated rom the Program prior to the Department being notified that the individual had a requirement to register as a sex offender.

enforcement notification was completed by USMS WITSEC Program personnel in September 2012.

We believe that notifying law enforcement officials of the presence of a sex offender in their community can mitigate the danger to the public while maintaining the overall security of the sex offender Program participant. Since the USMS is not required to monitor terminated Program participants, this provides law enforcement with the opportunity to mitigate the risks presented by such sex offenders who choose to relocate by sharing these individuals' whereabouts with other law enforcement agencies. We believe that in instances where security concerns ███, ███████████████████████████████████████, law enforcement notification ███████. We recommended in June 2014 that OEO finalize a written protocol that contains guidance to assist current and future OEO officials in determining whether or not to authorize law enforcement notification of sex offender Program participants. OEO's protocol, finalized in late July 2014, discusses law enforcement notification as a possible mitigation measure.

OEO and USMS Protocols

During our audit, we determined that prior to 2013 OEO and the USMS did not have formal protocols for the admission and vetting of sex offenders and for the handling and monitoring of sex offenders admitted into the Program. The USMS provided us with directives and standard operating procedures for the handling and monitoring of sex offenders admitted into the Program which had been marked as "under review" since 2007.[34] We were told that these procedures were superseded by a USMS Program policy directive issued in July 2013.[35] This directive stated, in part, that it was USMS policy to:

> "[P]rohibit a sex offender, ██████████████████ from entering into the Witness Security Program ... [and] will request termination of any Program participant who is either arrested for a sex offense or who subsequently becomes identified as a sex offender."

However, this USMS Program policy prohibiting the admission of any sex offender and requiring the termination of any Program participant that is arrested

---

[34] A USMS WITSEC Program official informed us that these policies and procedures were considered effective at the time of dissemination to Program personnel. The date of dissemination was unclear from the documents we were provided. One USMS WITSEC Program official informed us that even if a policy or procedure is labeled "under review," it is to be followed by WITSEC Program personnel, while another USMS official stated that USMS WITSEC Program personnel are not required to follow policies labeled "under review."

[35] In January 2014, OIG auditors were provided with an updated version of this policy that contained non-substantive revisions. The revised policy retained substantively similar language prohibiting sex offenders ██████████████ from entering the WITSEC Program. This prohibition is not present in the finalized version of the USMS WITSEC Program protocol that was finalized in September 2014.

for a sex offense was not aligned with OEO's policy. We understand, through our discussions with USMS personnel, that the USMS strongly believes that it is impossible   Program participant. However, OEO, not the SMS, has the authority to admit individuals into and terminate Program participants from the Program. Therefore, while a USMS preliminary interview and recommendation is part of the application and WITSEC Program admissions process, OEO may choose to admit a sex offender into the Program despite the USMS's protocol to the contrary. Likewise, it is within OEO's discretion to retain a sex offender in the Program despite the USMS's desires to remove a Program participant who is convicted of a sex offense while in the Program. Given their overlapping and interconnected responsibilities in connection with managing the Program, we believe that OEO and the USMS should have policies that are consistent with one another in this area.

In June and July 2014, we recommended that OEO and the USMS revise their policies to reflect consistent rules regarding admittance and termination decisions involving sex offenders. In September 2014, the USMS finalized a comprehensive protocol for the handling and monitoring of sex offenders admitted into the USMS WITSEC Program. In October 2014, a USMS official notified us that this finalized comprehensive protocol superseded the previous protocol prohibiting sex offenders from entering the Program, therefore this inconsistency is no longer an issue.

While OEO officials have stated that it would be rare for an individual convicted of a sex offense to be admitted into the Program, they have also stated that they will not prohibit an individual's admittance to the Program solely based on his or her status as a sex offender. We understand OEO's position to be that each case is unique and decisions must be made based on the specific circumstances involved and weighed against the potential value of the Program participant's cooperation with the Department. However, a protocol on participant admission decisions has important practical value. For example, in January 2014, the Director of OEO informed the OIG that the then-draft OEO protocol had been used to make an admittance decision regarding a prospective USMS Program participant ▮▮▮▮▮. After considering the admission materials and criteria in the then-draft protocol, the individual by OEO. We believe this is demonstrative of how a protocol can be useful to OEO officials in deciding whether or not to admit or retain a sex offender-witness in the Program.

In late July 2014, OEO provided the OIG with a finalized protocol, which included criteria to consider when determining whether a sex offender-witness should be admitted into the Program and whether a waiver of sex offender registration should be issued to sex offender Program participants. We recommended in October 2014 that OEO complete specific guidelines for whether or not to retain a Program participant who commits a sex offense ▮▮▮▮▮ while in the Program. OEO's updated finalized protocol from November 2014 includes a section specifically related to Program participants who are arrested for sex-related crimes.

Additionally, even though an individual may not have a conviction for a sex-related crime ███████████████████, OEO should still consider additional information, such as whether or not the individual was convicted of or pled to a lesser offense that ████████████████████████. For example, during our audit we learned that there was one individual who, prior to admission to the Program, was charged with Assault to Commit Rape. USMS personnel researched the disposition of the charge and learned that this person pled to a lesser offense that does not ██████████████████████. We believe that this information is important for OEO to consider in its decisions on admittance and mitigating measures, such as whether or not to authorize law enforcement notification, as well as assist the USMS in making decisions on the handling and monitoring of such individuals. We believe including this consideration in a written, finalized OEO protocol for the admission and vetting of sex offenders into the Program is important to ensure that future WITSEC Program officials also take this important information into consideration.

We recognize that both the WITSEC statute and the SORNA Guidelines allow for waiver of registration requirements. However, these statutes also encourage alternative arrangements, confirming that the intent is to provide for the safety of a protected witness while retaining public safety. In late June 2014, we recommended that OEO finalize written protocols that address any additional criteria beyond the statutory criteria for Program eligibility specific to sex offenders sponsored into the Program. We also recommended that these protocols address the process of deciding whether to retain a Program participant who commits a sex offense ███████████████ while in the Program. Furthermore, in July 2014 we recommended that the USMS finalize protocols to ensure the appropriate handling and monitoring of sex offenders admitted into the USMS WITSEC Program. As stated in earlier sections of this report, OEO and the USMS finalized protocols in late July and September 2014, respectively. These protocols addressed these concerns.

███████████████ **Terminated Program**
████████████████████████████████

To protect a Program participant, a new identity is generally provided to the individual when he or she enters the Program. If a Program participant has a criminal history, ████████████████████████████████
████████████████████████████████████

████████████████████████████████████
████████████████████████████████████
████████████████████████████████████

██
██ leaving both law enforcement officers and the public more vulnerable to criminal activity.

We spoke with ███████ USMS personnel regarding the current process used to notify the USMS ██
██
██
Program personnel would then review the information and inform ██
██
██
██. Regardless ████████
WITSEC Program personnel will continue to ████████████████████████.

In October 2014, a USMS official informed us that ████████████████
██
██
████████████████████████████████. This same official stated that the USMS is not responsible for monitoring and protecting terminated Program participants and this review creates additional work for the USMS WITSEC Program case management team.

_____

██
██
██
██

██

██

After being informed about the process of USMS ██████████████████████ , we inquired further about ██████████████████████████████████████ ████████████████████████████. In November 2014, the USMS informed us that 11,257 individuals have been admitted into the USMS WITSEC Program and provided with a new legal name but have an "inactive" status.[40] Of these 11,257 inactive Program participants, there are ████████████████████████ ██.

While not all of these individuals may have a criminal history, this means that there are at least ██████ terminated Program participants who were provided with new identities who are no longer regularly monitored by Program personnel and ████ ██ ██ ████████████[41] We believe this creates a loophole in the Program process, leaving law enforcement agencies unnecessarily uninformed and unable to utilize al available tools to perform their duties. For these reasons, we believe it is important that OEO ensure that these Program participants' ██████████████████████. Although the scope of our audit work focused on sex offenders in the Program, we believe the serious nature of the issues surrounding ████████████████ of all Program participants ██████████████ warranted an expansion of our audit scope to address this issue.

In January 2014, an OEO official explained that ████████████████████████ ████████████████████████████████████ cannot be unilaterally executed by USMS WITSEC Program personnel because it is a disclosure of Program information and, as such, requires the Director of OEO's authorization. This same official stated that an unwritten policy for determining whether to authorize the ██████████████ Program participant identity information was implemented in early 2012. He stated that this unwritten procedure requires USMS WITSEC Program personnel to recommend whether ██ ██████████████ in its request to OEO for both voluntary and involuntary termination of the participant from the Program. The OEO Director then decides ██████████████████████

---

[40] The population of "inactive" Program participants includes individuals who are deceased, have been deported, voluntarily terminated, or were involuntarily terminated.

The USMS informed us that there are 7,167 Program participants who did not receive a new name. According to the USMS, these 7,167 Program participants did not receive a new name because they: (1) were born after their parents' authorization into the Program; (2) only participated as a prisoner witness; (3) were authorized into the Program but had the authorization rescinded or otherwise decided not to enter the Program; (4) participated in a short term pilot Program in which new names were not provided; (5) were authorized into the Program prior to 1984 when Title 18 mandated name changes; (6) were authorized after October 20, 2014; or (7) were not given a new name for other reasons, such as the Program participant was not in the Program long enough to receive a new name. As of November 2014, there were 401 active Program participants who have been admitted into the Program and have received a new legal name from the USMS. However, 2 of these 401 active Program participants have ██ because they are currently prisoner witnesses.

[41] According to WITSEC Program policy ████████████████████████████████████ ██

22

███, with the presumption being to do so. This official further stated that two considerations are included in OEO's final decision: (1) the reason for the individual's removal from the Program; and (2) the Program participant's prior criminal history. These factors are both considered when assessing whether or not safety concerns exist both for the Program participant and the general public. The official stated that if a Program participant has a violent past, such as felony arrests and convictions, then OEO would likely authorize the USMS' ███.

Prior to late July 2014, there was no finalized WITSEC Program procedure for ███ once a participant is terminated from the Program, including sex offenders whose █████████████████████████ may have been waived. While we understand that the decision ██ helps to ensure a protected witness's safety, our concern relates to the process once a Program participant is terminated from the Program because USMS WITSEC Program personnel are not required to monitor these Program participants. We believe that without providing ███████████████████████████████████████ with complete information on these individuals, the risk exists that law enforcement will not have █████████████ to important information it needs to protect the public.

During our audit, we reviewed Program files and determined that at least one of the identified ███ had received a waiver of registration, and had been terminated from the Program approximately █ years ago and only recently ████████████████████████████████████.[42] Therefore, this sex offender went █████████, generally unmonitored, and ███████████████████████████████ for at least 10 years after being terminated from the Program. While one instance may not indicate a systemic problem, an unwritten policy increases the likelihood that this situation will recur. We believe all of the sex offenders ████████████████ and are terminated from the Program ████████████████████, when possible. In the alternative, we believe that ██. In November 2014, OEO and USMS officials stated that all identified sex offenders who were admitted into the WITSEC Program had been terminated from the Program and have ████████████████ ███.

In late June and early July 2014, we recommended that WITSEC Program officials finalize a protocol regarding the ███████████████████████████ ████████████ of terminated Program participants, including sex offender Program participants. In late July 2014, a protocol was finalized. The finalized protocol states that ██ ██

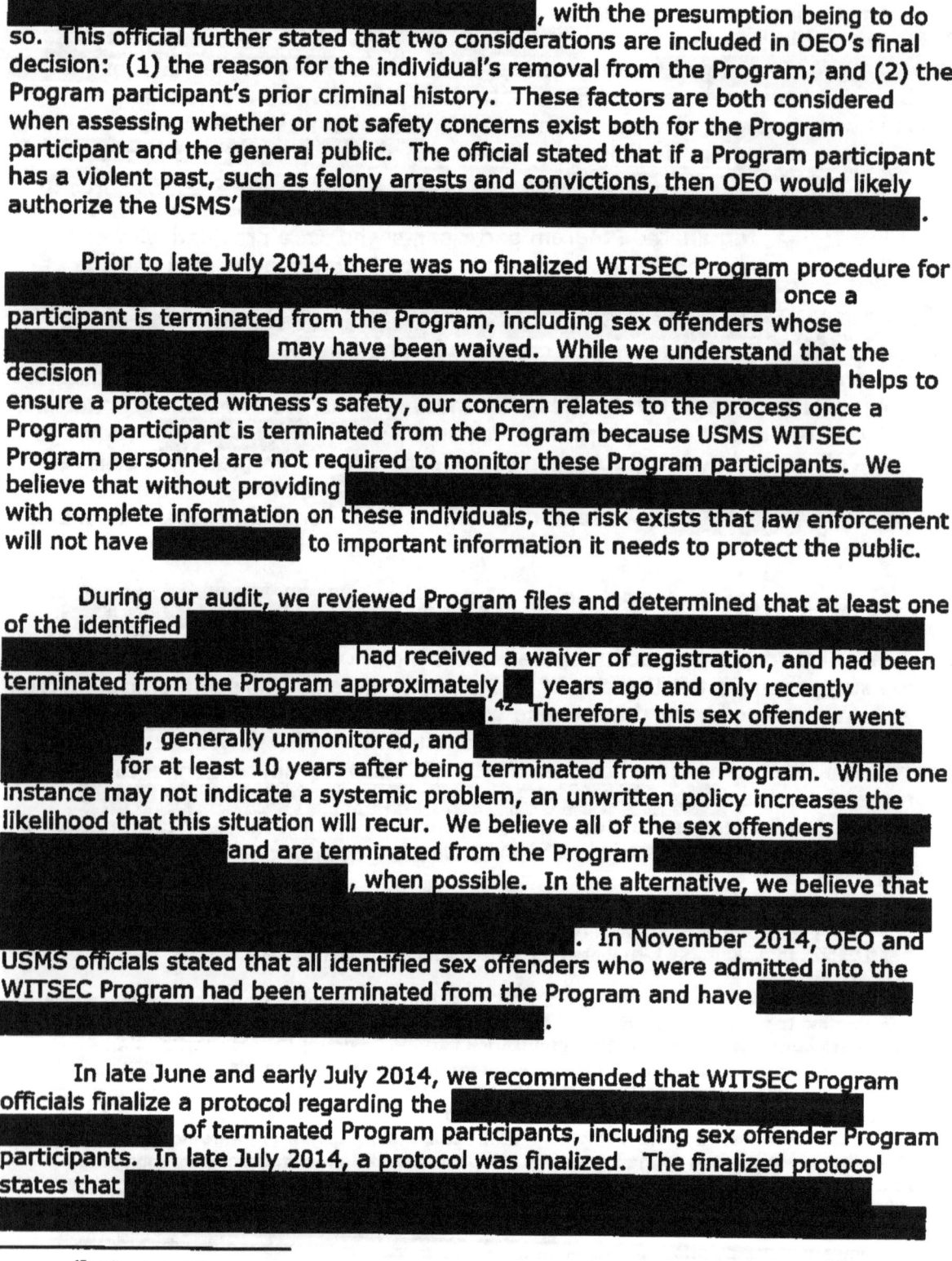

---

[42] The Department did not provide the dates of when the identity records for the identified sex offenders were █████████████████████████; it only confirmed ███████████████████████. We were provided information for when this individual's ███████████████████████████ through the Program file testing.

███████ is a form of disclosure and thus can only be authorized by the Attorney General or the Attorney General's designee, currently the Director of OEO. The protocol acknowledges a presumption in favor of ████████████████████ ██ can be overcome. Further, the protocol states that ████████████████████████████████ will be made on a case-by-case basis after looking at the circumstances and considering whether law enforcement or the public will be safer with disclosure versus any increased threat to the formerly protected Program participant. Specific factors listed for consideration include the terminated Program participant's criminal history, conduct while in the Program, and the level of any threat this individual poses to the public. If the OEO Director decides ████ ███████████████████████████████, a formal disclosure memorandum will be provided to USMS WITSEC Program personnel █████████████████████ ███████████████████████████ We believe this finalized protocol along with the ███████████████████ █████████ will help mitigate the risk of these individuals to law enforcement and to relocation communities.

Recommendations

We recommend that the Department:

1. Confirm that all sex offenders previously admitted into the Program ████ ██ ██ ████████████████████████████████████

2. Ensure that OEO and the USMS identify all individuals currently active in the Program who have been convicted of a sex-related crime in order to be in a position to properly mitigate the risks associated with these individuals.

STATEMENT ON INTERNAL CONTROLS

As required by the *Government Auditing Standards*, we tested, as appropriate, internal controls significant within the context of our audit objectives. A deficiency in an internal control exists when the design or operation of a control does not allow management or employees, in the normal course of performing their assigned functions, to prevent or detect in a timely manner: (1) impairments to the effectiveness and efficiency of operations, (2) misstatements in financial or performance information, or (3) violations of laws and regulations. Our evaluation of the internal controls of the Office of Enforcement Operations (OEO) and the U.S. Marshals Service (USMS) was not made for the purpose of providing assurance on their internal control structure as a whole. OEO and the USMS management are responsible for the establishment and maintenance of internal controls.

As noted in the Findings and Recommendations section of this report, we identified deficiencies in OEO and the USMS's internal controls that are significant within the context of the audit objectives. Based upon the audit work performed, we believe these identified deficiencies adversely affected OEO's ability to effectively make Program admission and notification decisions, such as ███████████ ██ to waive sex offender registration or notify law enforcement, for sex offenders sponsored into the Program. We found that, prior to July 2014, OEO lacked a written, finalized protocol relating to sex offender Program participants. On July 31, 2014, OEO finalized a protocol containing criteria for current and future OEO officials to use to determine whether or not: (1) to admit a sex offender into the Program; (2) to issue a waiver of sex offender registration; and (3) to notify law enforcement of a sex offender's relocation to a community. Additionally, we believe that other deficiencies we identified affected the USMS's ability to effectively handle and monitor sex offenders admitted into the Program. We found that the USMS did not have a finalized protocol pertaining to the handling and monitoring of sex offenders admitted into the Program until September 2014.

Because we are not expressing an opinion on OEO and the USMS's internal control structure as a whole, this statement is intended solely for the information and use of OEO and the USMS. This restriction is not intended to limit the distribution of this report, which is a matter of public record. However, we are limiting the distribution of this report because it contains sensitive information that must be appropriately controlled.[43]

---

[43] A redacted copy of this report with sensitive information removed will be made available publicly.

STATEMENT ON COMPLIANCE WITH LAWS AND REGULATIONS

As required by the *Government Auditing Standards*, we tested, as appropriate given our audit scope and objectives, selected transactions, records, procedures, and practices, to obtain reasonable assurance that the Office of Enforcement Operations (OEO) and the U.S. Marshals Services' (USMS) management complied with federal laws and regulations for which noncompliance, in our judgment, could have a material effect on the results of our audit. OEO and the USMS' management are responsible for ensuring compliance with federal laws and regulations applicable to the Department of Justice. In planning our audit, we identified the following laws and regulations that concerned the operations of the auditee and that were significant within the context of the audit objectives:

- 18 U.S.C. § 3521 (2006).
- 42 U.S.C. § 14071, as amended (1994).
- 42 U.S.C. § 16901 (2006).
- 28 C.F.R. 0.111b (2001).
- 28 C.F.R. Part 72 (2007).

Our audit included examining, on a test basis, OEO and the USMS' compliance with the aforementioned laws and regulations, and whether non-compliance could have a material effect on OEO and the USMS' operations. We did so by interviewing auditee personnel, assessin   internal control procedures, reviewing case files, verifying   , and examining procedural practices for the admission, han ing, an   monitoring of sex offender-witnesses admitted into the Program.

Nothing came to our attention that caused us to believe that OEO or the USMS were not in compliance with the aforementioned laws and regulations.

AUDIT OBJECTIVES, SCOPE, AND METHODOLOGY

Objectives

The objectives of this audit were to evaluate the Department's:
(1) admission and vetting of sex offenders into the WITSEC Program; (2) handling, tracking, and monitoring of sex offenders who were admitted into the USMS WITSEC Program; and (3) procedures for notifying states, local municipalities, and other law enforcement agencies regarding the relocation of sex offenders.

Scope and Methodology

We conducted this performance audit in accordance with generally accepted government auditing standards. Those standards require that we plan and perform the audit to obtain sufficient, appropriate evidence to provide a reasonable basis for our findings and conclusions based on our audit objectives. We believe that the evidence obtained provides a reasonable basis for our findings and conclusions based on our audit objectives.

To accomplish our objectives, we performed fieldwork related to this high risk group at OEO, USMS Headquarters, and the USMS Safe Site Orientation Center to determine how OEO and USMS personnel balance the safety of the public with the protection and security of the witness Specifically, we:

- interviewed OEO and USMS personnel;

- performed a review of USMS and OEO draft and finalized policies and procedures; and

- performed a review for 21 of the 47 USMS and OEO WITSEC Program files for which the witness or their famil member had been identified by the Department as   as a sex offender as of July 2013.

In July 2013, the Department provided the OIG with three lists containin the names of a total of 47 individuals it had identified as ▓▓▓▓▓▓ sex offenders and who had been admitted into the Program.   e irst list contained information for eight individuals who the Department determined were sex offenders at the time they were authorized into the Program. The second list contained information for eight individuals who the Department identified as having been convicted of a sex offense while in the Program, ▓▓▓▓▓▓▓▓▓ ▓▓▓▓▓▓▓▓▓▓▓. Finally, the third list contained information for 31 individuals who were identified by the Department as havin   been convicted of a sex offense after being terminated from the Program,   .

We used these 3 lists to select a judgmental sample of 21 OEO and USMS WITSEC Program files of sex offender-witnesses for testing. These 21 files included all 8 of the individuals who were sex offenders at the time of Program authorization, all 8 individuals who were convicted of a sex offense ████████████████ while in the Program, and 5 of the 31 files for indivi ua s who were convicted of a sex offense after being either voluntaril   or involuntaril terminated from the Program, since 1993, ███████████.[44] Our sampling design and met o o ogy   oes not permit us to project our results to the universe from which we selected our sample.

The above numbers were used at the time of the file review sample selection in July 2013 and the onsite review of the selected files was completed by the end of August 2013. However, in October 2013, after the completion of our file review, the Department provided the OIG with some updated information, including the addition of a terminated Program participant to the list of identified Program participants who were convicted of a sex offense   while in the Program. We did not review the USMS and OEO Program files for this newly identified individual because this individual was listed as deceased. In May 2014 the Department provided updated lists of the identified sex offenders admitted into the WITSEC Program. These updated lists contained 47 total individuals: 7 individuals who were convicted of sex offenses prior to admission into the Program   , 9 individuals who were convicted of sex offenses during Program participation, and 31 individuals who were convicted of sex offenses after termination from the Program. One individual was removed by the Department from the list of individuals identified as havin   been convicted of a sex offense   rior to Program authorization   .

Approximately 1 year after the initiation of this audit, in July 2014, the Department provided another batch of u dated lists which contained a total of 58 individuals convicted of sex offenses   : 10 individuals who were convicted of sex offenses prior to a mission into t e Program, 10 individuals who were convicted of sex offenses during Program participation, and 38 individuals who were convicted of sex offenses after termination from the Program. The WITSEC Program files for these additional 11 Program participants were not reviewed because it was determined to be too late in the audit process to do so. Furthermore, the three additional individuals identified as havin   been convicted of sex offenses prior to admission into the Program   all had sex offense convictions from the 1960's, entered into the Program, and were then terminated from the Program in the 1980's. Therefore, these individuals were outside of the 20 year time period established for reviewing the files of individuals

---

[44] One participant is currently incarcerated in state prison serving a life sentence. The general notes related to this participant state that this individual will not be offered relocation upon release. Therefore, the audit team did not test this file.

identified as having been convicted of a sex offense after being either voluntarily or involuntarily terminated from the Program.

DEPARTMENT OF JUSTICE RESPONSE

~~LAW ENFORCEMENT SENSITIVE~~

U.S. Department of Justice

Criminal Division

Assistant Attorney General   *Washington, D.C 20530*

January 29, 2015

MEMORANDUM

To: Jason R. Malmstrom
             Acting Assistant Inspector General for Audit
             U.S. Department of Justice

From: Paul M. O'Brien
             Deputy Assistant Attorney General
             Criminal Division

             William Snelson
             Associate Director for Operations
             United States Marshals Service

Subject: Department of Justice's Response to the Office of the Inspector General's Draft
             Audit Report entitled *Audit of the Department of Justice's Handling of Sex
             Offenders in the Federal Witness Security Program* (January 2015)

Thank you for the opportunity to respond to the Office of the Inspector General's 2015
draft audit report entitled *Audit of the Department of Justice's Handling of Sex Offenders in the
Federal Witness Security Program* (*OIG Audit Report*). The Department appreciates the OIG's
role in periodically auditing the federal Witness Security Program (WitSec Program), and
believes that, through our combined efforts, the Program has undergone significant
improvements since the OIG first audited the Program in September 1993.

The *OIG Audit Report* contains two recommendations aimed at mitigating the safety risk
posed to the public by current and former WitSec Program participants who are sex offenders.
The Department concurs with both recommendations. As detailed below, we believe that we
have fully implemented those recommendations and respectfully request that they be closed.

I.   **The Department will Continue to Consider the Admission of Sex Offender
         Program Applicants Only in Extraordinary Cases**

For over forty years, the WitSec Program has enabled the Government to bring to justice
the most violent and dangerous criminals by providing critical protection for witnesses and their
families fearing for their safety. The WitSec Program has successfully protected over 18,000

participants—including innocent victim-   and cooperating defendants and their dependents—from intimidation and retribution. This vital and effective prosecution tool allows the Government to protect witnesses   assistance is necessary as part of criminal investigations and whose testimony is critical to secure convictions in federal and state courts.

Prior to being admitted into the Program, all witnesses—including convicted sex offenders—are subjected to an intensive vetting process. Witnesses are admitted into the Program only if, and after, the sponsoring law enforcement agency, the sponsoring United States Attorney and the United States Marshals Service (USMS) provide detailed information and assessments to the Criminal Division's Office of Enforcement Operations (OEO) to support its determination   the witness and family members are suitable for the Program and the need to admit the witness and family members outweighs the risk to the public and the relocation community. See 18 U.S.C. § 3521(c). Of note, no witness ever has been admitted into the WitSec Program and provided with relocation services in connection with their conviction of a sex offense. Rather, the limited number of convicted sex offenders have been   into the Program and provided with relocation services as a result of them being a witness or related to a witness of a serious offense or organized crime. See 18 U.S.C. § 3521(a)(1).

The Department agrees with the *OIG Audit Report* that the admission of witnesses or witnesses'   y members who were previously convicted of sex offenses into the relocation portion of the WitSec   raises significant public safety concerns. For this reason, it has been the Department's policy to provide relocation services to individuals convicted of sex offenses only in extraordinary situations. In 2011, Department officials reaffirmed this position and established a policy that there was a presumption that sex offenders would not be offered relocation services. As discussed below, in the history of the WitSec Program, only ten individuals—out of over 18,000 participants—were admitted into the Program and provided with relocation services after having been convicted of a sex offense. Notably, no current Program participant   In addition, none of those individuals is currently exempted by the Department

As a public safety measure, Congress and states sought to increase awareness among both law enforcement and the general public by imposing registration requirements for sex offenders in many cases of conviction. See 42 U.S.C. § 16901 *et seq.* (Sex Offender Registration and Notification Act (SORNA)). In passing the witness relocation and protection statute, however, Congress recognized that there could be circumstances in which protected witnesses would need to be exempted from registration. For this reason, Congress provided the Department with the authority to waive sex offender registration requirements for Program participants. See 18 U.S.C. § 3521(b)(1)(H), (d)(3); 73 Fed. Reg. 38030, 38032 (July 2, 2008) (final guidelines to interpret and implement SORNA include the Attorney General's authority to waive the sex offender registration requirement for certain Program participants); *see also* DOJ National Guidelines for Sex Offender Registration and Notification (July 2008), Section IV(E).

In the history of the Program, the Department has used this waiver provision judiciously—waiving the sex offender registration requirement only four times. Notably, the last

2

waiver that the Department granted was in 2007. In the limited instances in which waivers were granted, the Program Director at the time decided that issuing the waivers was necessary to protect the witnesses or family members. Waivers were granted after a determination that the witnesses provided significant information to law enforcement officials which was critical in securing convictions in important cases. In determining that the waivers were appropriate, the Program Director concluded that the need for the witnesses' testimony outweighed the risk of danger to the public. As noted in the *OIG Audit Report*, in the history of the Program, no sex offender who was admitted and granted a waiver of sex offender registration ever committed a new sex offense while in the Program.

Importantly, all four of these waivers ████████████ The Department████████ ████████—one of the waiver recipients had ██████ been terminated from the Program; two other recipients decided to voluntarily terminate from the Program. The fourth waiver recipient was identified as a sex offender in March 2013 from a manual review of OEO files. Although this individual had been terminated from the Program in 2003, the Department ████████████████

Regarding the six other sex offenders who were admitted into the Program, the Department admitted five of those individuals prior to the passage of sex offender registration legislation. All five of those individuals were removed from the Program prior to or within same year as the passage of the Wetterling Act in 1994—the statute that established guidelines for states to track sex offenders. The final sex offender who was admitted into the Program was admitted after the passage of the Wetterling Act the Adam Walsh Act. At the time of admission,
████████near   two years   remo   pursuant to review
Department,
The Department

As demonstrated by practice in accordance with policy, the Department believes that the potential admission of a sex offender into the WitSec Program—and, in particular, the potential waiver of a registration requirement for a convicted sex offender—mandates a high level of scrutiny. The Department will continue to consider the admission of such applicants only in extraordinary cases.

II.

In November 2014, OEO implemented protocols which formalized the presumption against admitting sex offenders ████████████████████into the Program, due to the risks to the public of waiving the sex offender registration requirement. The protocols include additional criteria to be considered in deciding whether to grant a waiver of the sex offender registration requirement. The additional criteria increase the scrutiny placed on sex offender above   beyond the extensive vetting that always takes place prior to the admission

3

of an applicant into the Program.

In addition, in the rare circumstance when the Program Director determines that a convicted sex offender ███████████████████████ has overcome the presumption against acceptance ███████████████ protocols mandate heightened scrutiny of that decision. According to the protocols, prior to making a final authorizing decision, the Program Director must consult with both the USMS Assistant Director for Witness Security and the Deputy Assistant Attorney General of the Criminal Division with oversight responsibilities for OEO. Also, in the unlikely event that a convicted sex offender is ██████ into the Program, as described in the *OIG Audit Report* the USMS has implemented protocols for the handling and monitoring of sex offender Program participants.

The *OIG Audit Report* notes that another ten individuals were convicted of sex offenses while in the Program. The Program provides participants with no immunity, and those individuals were terminated from the Program and held accountable for their criminal conduct. The *OIG Audit Report* also notes that there were thirty-eight individuals who were convicted of sex offenses after they left the Program. The Department has confirmed ███████████████ for twenty-four of these former Program participants—the remaining fourteen individuals are ████████ incarcerated, or have been ██████████ from the United States. Additionall ██ concerns.

S████████y, the Department has ██████ extensive efforts to mitigate public safety concerns by developing procedures and policies ████████████████████████ when a Program participant leaves or is ████████████████ gram. ████y Department implemented a policy of requiring Program officials to consider whether a terminated Program participant's ███████████████████ ██████████████████████ when they leave the program. At the time of termination, USMS personnel recommend to OEO whether a participant' ███████████████████████████████████ ████████ The OEO Director then determines whether to authorize ███████████████████████████ ████████ operating under a presumption that the Program participant's ████████████████████ This was an important change to protocols which significantly mitigates the safety risk to the public.

III. ██ ,

Through our engagement with the OIG during this audit, the Department believes that we have fully implemented both of the OIG's recommendations. First, the OIG advised that the Department should ensure that all sex offenders ████ously admitted into the ████████

Department has ████████ that: (a) ████ sex ██████████ previously admitted into the Program have ██████ and (b

Second, the OIG   that the Department ensure that OEO and the USMS identify all individuals currently   ·   in the Program who have been convicted of sex-related crimes, regardless of ████████████████ The Department has identified all such individuals, including by conducting a review of all Program case files and ████████████████ comparisons with ██████████████████████ After completing a hand-review of over 18,000 files, which resulted in the identification of sex offenders ████████████████████ the Department also identified four active Program participants convicted of sex crimes

                                                                    aware
steps to mitigate any public safety concerns.

In closing, the Department believes that we have fully implemented the recommendations in the *OIG Audit Report* and, accordingly, we respectfully request that the recommendations be closed. The Department agrees that the changes recommended by the OIG were necessary, will ensure the WitSec Program's continued vitality in protecting witnesses and their family members, and will provide additional security to the public.

FFICE OF THE INSPECTOR GENERAL ANALYSIS AND SUMMARY OF ACTIONS NECESSARY TO CLOSE THE AUDIT REPORT

The Office of the Inspector General (OIG) provided a draft of th's audit report to the United States Marshals Service (USMS), the Office of Enforcement Operations (OEO) and the Office of the Deputy Attorney General (ODAG). The Department's response is incorporated in Appendix 2 of this report. The following provides the OIG analysis of the Department's response and summary of actions necessary to close the report

Analysis of Response

In response to our audit report, the Department concurred with our recommendations and discussed the actions it has implemented in response to our findings. As a result, we consider the report to be resolved.

Although the Department agreed w'th our recommendations and acknowledged that the changes recommended by the OIG were necessary, its response incorporated a broader analysis rather than simply limiting the discussion to our two recommendations. Therefore, we address the Department's discussion in the following paragraphs.

Throughout its response, the Department referred to sex offenders that were admitted into the WITSEC program in a very broad sense. However, the Department clearly defines a sex offender WITSEC Program participant as "an individual who was authorized for relocation and name change services, who, prior to authorization, was convicted of a sex offense ███ ███████████████████████████████████████ " Therefore, we applied the Department's definition of a sex offender Program participant throughout our report, including this analysis, and refer to this group of individuals as "████████████████████████████████████." However, there may be individuals who were convicted of sex-related crimes ████████████ ████████████ in the state of conviction or state of relocation who have been admitted into the Program. As we state in our report, given the nature of the WITSEC Program, we believe that individuals convicted of sex-related crimes that ████████████████████████ pose risks that the Department needs to take into account and address.

In addition, the Department stated in its response: "[a]s noted in the *OIG Audit Report*, in the history of the Program, no sex offender who was admitted and granted a waiver of sex offender registration ever committed a new sex offense while in the Program." However, this was not our statement. It is not possible for us to conclude that a sex offender Program participant, who was granted a waiver, never committed a new sex offense while in the Program. Rather, our report states that we did not identify any instances during the course of our audit where a sex offender Program participant who received a waiver of sex offender registration was convicted of a new sex offense while in the WITSEC Program. We believe that waivers only provide the Program participants with protections, not the public, because those individuals are not required to adhere to legally mandated safeguards or preventative measures. As stated in our report, we believe that the Department generally did not utilize safeguards to protect and notify the public and law enforcement about the risk these individuals posed during the time period   .

Since we began our initial review of the WITSEC Program in October 2011, which addressed known or suspected terrorist Program participants, the Department has made a concerted effort to address issues that arise during the course of our reviews and incorporate necessary changes in its policies and procedures. For example, the Department's response noted the creation of a policy in 2011 that presupposes sex offenders would not be offered relocation services. Likewise, in its response, the Department stated that it ███████████████████████████████ in October 2012 and one in March 2013.

Since the initiation of this portion of the WITSEC audit in July 2013 related to sex offenders, the Department's efforts to improve the management and oversight of the Program have included finalizing a policy addressing the presumption that sex offenders will not be offered relocation services, finalizing policies and procedures for the handling and monitoring of Program participants ████████████████████████████ or who have been convicted of sex-related offenses, and finalizing a policy requiring Program officials to consider whether terminated Program participants' identity information ██████████████████████████████ when they leave the Program. These corrective actions have remedied deficiencies that existed in the WITSEC Program when we began our audit, and we commend the Department for making these important improvements. The following discusses our analysis of the Department's response to recommendations that we made in this report.

Recommendations:

1. **Confirm that all sex offenders previously admitted into the Program** ██ ██

    Resolved. The Department concurred with our recommendation. The Department further requested closure of this recommendation based on their confirmation that (a) all sex offenders previously admitted into the Program ███████████████████████████████████████ ██ ████████████████████████████████ This recommendation can be closed when the Department provides documentation supporting its stated actions.

2. **Ensure that OEO and the USMS identify all individuals currently active in the Program who have been convicted of a sex-related crime in order to be in a position to properly mitigate the risks associated with these individuals.**

    Resolved. The Department concurred with our recommendation to identify all individuals currently active in the Program who have been convicted of sex-related crimes, regardless of registration requirements and requested that this recommendation be closed based on the actions it has taken to satisfy the recommendation. The Department stated that it has identified all such individuals by performing computer comparisons ████████████████████████ ████████ as well as a hand-review of over 18,000 files. The Department stated its file review identified four active Program participants who were convicted of sex crimes that do not require registration under the laws of the states in which they reside, work, or attend school. The Department further stated that USMS WITSEC Program personnel have taken steps to mitigate any public safety concerns related to these individuals.

    This recommendation can be closed when we obtain documentation relating to the four individuals the Department referred to in its response to this recommendation. In addition, please provide us with documentation reflecting the steps taken by the Department to mitigate any public safety concerns posed by these four individuals.

The Department of Justice Office of the Inspector General
(DOJ OIG) is a statutorily created independent entity
whose mission is to detect and deter waste, fraud,
abuse, and misconduct in the Department of Justice, and
to promote economy and efficiency in the Department's
operations. Information may be reported to the DOJ
OIG's hotline at www.justice.gov/oig/hotline or
(800) 869-4499.